Her Story
Our Story

Different Faces
Same Trauma

True Stories of Triumph

Presented By Stephanie Wall

To Aunt Libby
Thanks
Paula for a future!
Tell your story!

Printed in the United States of America

ISBN: 9798732240511

Contact Info:
Stephanie Wall
Speakerstephanie.com (website)
Speakerstephaniew (Instagram

Dedication

I dedicate this book to women who seek to break barriers to self-esteem, to live, love, and create a legacy in their families and communities...on their journey to rediscovery.

It gives me great pleasure to dedicate this book to my late mom, Odessa Dorsey-Johnson, and the late Mary Owens. Although, each of you received your wings several years ago, I miss you dearly. The great motivational speaker, Les Brown, often says, "Somethings are taught, and some things are caught." It may not have always appeared so, but I was listening, and I received the lessons taught, and I caught some that I didn't even know were lessons.

To the excellent contributors of this book: Pam, Sharon, Saprina, Sasha, Katrina, Hope, and the families and friends of these courageous contributors. I honor each of you. I dedicate this book to your families for their unwavering support during this process and your commitment to helping create a legacy.

We dedicate this book to all the courageous humans who have shared their stories to help another person make it past their pain. Some of you may have written books, shared it on a stage as speakers, or simply shared it in a private conversation. We see you, and we honor you.

To my husband, Kurt Wall, and our sons Kenard, Daevon & Kurt Jr., each of you have been my inspiration for moving forward with my dreams. I am super proud and thankful for all your support.

To my friend & mentor, Gloria Mayfield Banks, you have been the driving force for many other women. I am so grateful for our friendship and that God saw fit to place you not only in my path but as a permanent fixture in my life. I honor you for never giving up on me and always telling me what I needed to hear, not what I wanted to hear.

To my coach & publisher, Vanessa Collins. Your gentle spirit reminds me of my mother. Thank you for guiding us along on this journey. This project is a success due in part to you and your professional staff. Your ability to ask all of the right questions to get a greater understanding of what it is that I needed most is unmatched. I honor you.

Table of Contents

Thank You...

for purchasing this book. As my gift to you, please visit **https://bit.ly/HSOSBONUS** to get your special gift.

Also, please don't forget to leave a review on Amazon.

★ ★ ★ ★ ★

It takes courage to grow up and be who you really are.

E.E. CUMMINGS

Foreword

I know what an individual who has the spirit to win and seeks to help others to lean into their gifts looks like and how they operate. The Visionary, Stephanie Wall, is one of those individuals. To be asked to share my thoughts as the foreword for this book was an honor. I encourage you to take this opportunity to be impacted by Stephanie and the Co-Authors. Stephanie's light shines so brightly because of the way she manages her outlook, despite her journey, which was extremely hard and challenging.

It is no surprise that she shifts and builds others' mindsets because she understands they can have ALL they image for themselves and more. Being such a close friend, I know for a fact that her book can be a defining moment if you allow her journey, her experience, and her training to spark growth, which will make staying the same or going back to yesterday become impossible. She has brought six amazing women along with her on this journey. Each has shared a piece of who they are. Their stories will leave you on the edge of your seats and cause you to move closer to your unstoppable passion.

An unstoppable passion drives me to see others create their NEXT unapologetically. In this book, you will read page after page of examples of tenacity, power, and unstoppable spirits that wanted more and ones that would not let the environment or circumstances keep them from what they are predestined to have or do. If you have a dream sitting in your heart, these true stories will inspire you to move forward.

Gloria Mayfield Banks

Visit my website @ https://www.gloriamayfieldbanks.com/

Introduction

One day, I was drafting my notes and preparing to write a book that I just knew would change the lives of the women that I serve and seek to serve. Several days in a row, during my morning meditation, the title, "***Her Story Our Story, Same Trauma Different Faces***," kept popping up. You see, we all have a story. Those stories direct who we believe that we are and how we show up in the world. It takes extraordinary courage to look within and evaluate how those stories affect our daily lives. Master/International Personal Development Coach Bob Proctor says, *"Change is inevitable; personal development is a choice."* Whether you are a stay-at-home Mom, CEO, Elected Official, Public Servant, Service Worker, Medical Professional, or Educator, you have a story.

This book is for everyone and I knew from the start that the voices that needed to be heard were not necessarily mine. The Co-Authors in this book come from varying walks of life and live in different parts of the world. They join me, and many others, in being a part of a group that no one wants to be a part of. They are survivors of life's difficult seasons and moments.

Moving towards your dreams and goals can be scary. Especially when you have voices of self-doubt (the

Committee) talking in your head, telling you that you are not good enough for whatever it is that you want. The Contributors in this book are baring their truths so that you can be free to tell yours and know that you are not alone. They have conquered everything imaginable. Many of them have launched businesses, despite the physical pain and pasts riddled with incidents that they are not proud of, and yet still, they rise.

These women decided to take a chance on themselves, step out of their comfort zones, break-barriers to their self-esteem, and put pen to paper (type) sharing their TRUE stories of Triumph. As they each learned, what happened did not happen to them, but FOR them to grow. Each day they face uncertainty as we navigate one of the most unprecedented times in human history, specifically, a health pandemic and a social justice pandemic causing loss of life and social contact, because they understand that legacy is on the other side of their fears (false, evidence, appearing, real).

I am so excited to present: **Her Story Our Story-Different Faces, Same Trauma: Stories of Triumph;** an empowering compilation of stories from 6 EXTRAordinary women. Each experienced extreme cases of adversity. We take the journey with them through their lessons and losses as they learned to lift as they climbed. You will find your story or hope to move towards your

> *"Your STORY is about YOU, but it aint' FOR YOU."*
> **Dr. Cheryl Wood**

goals & dreams to create a legacy for you, your family, and community.

These co-authors are just like you. They are wives, mothers, daughters, friends, humans, people of faith, sisters, aunts, and granddaughters. Each story is a reminder that behind the eyes, there truly is a story. The significant part is that we all have an account. The hard part is we ALL have a tale....and it may be holding us back from being the best version of ourselves.

> *"I've learned that people will forget what you said, people will forget what you did, but people will never forget how you made them feel."*
> **Maya Angelou**

Her Story, Our Story is filled with stories of overcoming, tenacity, resilience, love, and so much more that will cause you to re-evaluate yourself. It will provide steps and affirm your decision to do it now. They will share how to get unstuck and become unstoppable. These 6 Co-Authors, did it afraid. Don't think for one second that they did not experience moments of self-doubt. Some of you may be inspiring speakers, coaches, or entrepreneurs that provide other services. The one thing that keeps leaders, entrepreneurs, managers, and those who serve others from becoming great is the lack of self-worth, self-fulfillment, self-determination, and self-esteem.

As you take the journey of discovery through reading each chapter, I challenge you to complete the suggested actions steps and spend time on the reflection questions. Change is truly possible, especially if you put in the work.

Stephanie Wall
Visionary of "Her Story Our Story, Same Trauma Different Faces: Stories of Triumph
Co-Author of Best Sellers, International Empowerment Speaker & Personal Development Coach

> *"We should always have three friends in our lives. One who walks ahead who we look up to and follow; one who walks beside us, who is with us every step of our journey; and then, one who we reach back for and bring along after we've cleared the way."*
> **Michelle Obama**

Divorce, Death, Depression & Still, I Smile

Pamela Alfred

Have you ever smiled when you were hurting inside? As a child, I smiled no matter how I felt. It was how I coped with the situations that were going on in my life. I found out the hard way that when you try to keep everything inside and plaster a smile on your face, it will eventually show back up at the worst time. In my case, it was always with a flood of tears.

I was born in Baltimore, Maryland and raised in the suburbs of Columbia. Most people assumed that because we lived in one of the wealthiest counties in the state, that we must be rich. Unfortunately, our family was considered low-income by all standards of measurement by the government. We were rich in community and family, but not financially. We lived in subsidized housing, which you might not have known right away if you were not from the community. For me, growing up in Columbia was great. Yes, we lived in poverty, but I had great friends, some of which did not live as we did. My childhood was not unique, despite its challenges. We had our ups and downs, boy crushes, fights, break-ups, and heartaches. The other kids used to tease us about where we lived and all the other things that come with living in poverty. Kids can be mean, especially when they are hurting inside too. Our extended family was always there to comfort and support me.

One day, my childhood boyfriend shows up at our house. We had been so-called dating (as the older adults used to say) through middle school and I had not seen him in seven years. Initially, I was kind of shocked. I did not know how to feel. He shared with me that he told his friends that he was going to get his middle school girlfriend. He was kind of quiet, like I was back then and I was not used to hearing him express himself like that. His words made me happy. At 18 years old, I felt loved for the very first time. A year later, we began talking about marriage. I was excited and nervous about the thought of leaving poverty behind and having my dream of a family with a husband, children, and a home with a white picket fence. One year later, we were married on October 23, 1987.

> *"The human spirit is stronger than anything that can happen to it."*
> **George C. Scott**

Marriage is work and adjusting to living with someone else is not easy. Being young made it even more challenging. This marriage challenged who I was to the core. I never did get that house with the picket fence. I became pregnant with our oldest son not long after. Life took a severe turn while I was pregnant. My husband was involved with drugs, and as a result, our house was raided by the local authorities. He was sentenced to several years in jail. I, like many of you reading this, tried to keep my family together. I accepted collect calls, sent pictures and money to him. After three years of his incarceration, our marriage ended in divorce. Going through the divorce was a very traumatic time of my life. I thought it could not get any worse.

I found myself in the one place that I dreaded. I was a single mom raising my two sons without their father. The thought of sleeping alone in my bed haunted me because being a wife and Mom was all I ever wanted to be. Sleeping alone felt like I failed as a wife. My kids and I slept in the living room of our two-bedroom Condo, for six months. I loved that Condo. I was so thrilled when we found a beautiful rental, and it was a condominium. Months later, my doctor told me that I was suffering from postpartum depression. After some time, we found our new normal.

I am going to pause here. If you or someone you love are experiencing any of the things that I experienced, here is some food-for-thought:

- Trust your gut.
- Only YOU can make YOU happy.
- Love should not hurt.
- Seek help when you cannot get out of bed for more than 24 hrs.
- It is okay not to be okay.

After a little time, I begin hanging out and I met a guy. He asked me to dance, and we danced for what seemed like hours. I had forgotten how it felt to be the center of someone's attention. We had a whirlwind year of dating. We made plans to introduce our children, and he proposed to me three years later at a baseball banquet surrounded by family and friends. We married one year later, September 5, 1998. Our wedding was a fairy tale come true and I felt just like a queen. There were three hundred people that attended our wedding. Everything was falling into place. At least, that is what I thought. Both of us had been married before. We purchased our first home, and I was so proud.

I even started my own home-based business called "Pamela's Playland of Learning." For years, I had worked in various daycare centers. The county provided financial aid for working parents to help pay for daycare. On one occasion, when I went to pick up the funds given for our boys, the worker said: "You could become a Day Care Provider. You could be collecting this money." I asked a few questions, took some courses at the Community College, and launched my business. Again, I was so proud. For a while, things were going well. Then, there seemed to be one significant loss after another. One night, I received a phone call that dad had suffered a heart attack. Sitting in the hospital, watching our dad on life support was so painful. My dad passed away weeks later with my sisters and me standing by his bedside, watching him take his last breath. I felt so many emotions. A familiar heaviness was beginning to creep its way back in. To add to the drama, my husband and I were not communicating well with each other. As time went on, things got worse. Our mom's health was now declining. A few months later, I was in the kitchen preparing breakfast for my preschoolers and infants when my phone rang, and my sister informed me that mom was rushed to the hospital and was on life support. Entering the hospital to see my mom lying in bed lifeless felt unreal. It was so hard sitting in the hospital watching another parent fight for their life.

We had to say our farewells on Thanksgiving morning, 2007. I watched my mom take her last breath and felt like I had taken mine. After her passing, I was a shell of the person that I was in the early years. I went into a deep depression that I thought was a secret. I could not pull myself back together mentally or emotionally. My marriage suffered; we both had checked out of it. I did not handle it well. I tried to drink the pain away. I knew that I needed help, but I just continued this downward spiral for months. While lying in bed one day, I said to myself, "I know there is light at the end of this tunnel". The next day I started googling therapist and within a week, I scheduled my first appointment. Making this appointment was not easy for me because I believed that saying "what happens in your house stays in your house." I was diagnosed with depression, and I discovered that I had not grieved my parents' deaths. I cried a river in that office. I left that first visit drained and confused, but happy with the strength to make my next appointment. I had several more visits. I could finally see my light coming back. Why do I share all of this? I share because I know that there

> "*You will lose someone you can't live without, and your heart will be badly broken, and the bad news is that you never completely get over the loss of your beloved. But this is also the good news.*"
> **Anne Lamott**

are women out there just like me. They have experienced so much pain & shame that they don't recognize themselves. They most likely feel that they are the only ones going through what they are going through. I share my story so that they can be free. I share so that I can be free. My story sat inside of me. The fear of it being fully out has kept me locked in a state of shame and fear. I give it away.

Les Brown says, "What other people have to say about you is none of your business."

Life does go on. I had some rough patches. I went through some periods that I am not proud. Since those early days, I have done a lot of self-development. I realize that I still have work to do because all that I have experienced occurred over time, and it will take time and commitment to work through some of it.

Psychology Today says:

Loneliness is as tied to the quality of one's relationships as it is to the number of connections one has. And it doesn't only stem from heartache or isolation. A lack of authenticity in relationships can result in feelings of loneliness. For some, not having a coveted animal companion or the absence of quiet presence in the home (even if one has plenty of social contacts in the wider world) can trigger loneliness.

I later met what we like to call a guy from down South (since Maryland is technically a Southern State). As seems to be the trend, I had a whirlwind courtship. I decided to move to Georgia with him and relocating was a big move for me. I almost talked myself out of moving on several occasions. I delayed the action for a year because of the pending birth of my first grand twins. I loved my boyfriend, but I had a hard time adjusting. I missed my family, and I felt lost in my new surroundings. After four months, I got a job, an administration position, at a local insurance training school. The company took a chance on me thanks to a referral from a good friend. The executive administrator was an excellent trainer. She trained me on how to use the software, telephone, and the inner workings of the business and I began to meet new friends, finding a new sense of strength.

I began working with a Life Coach. She worked with me on my self-esteem and "Choosing Me." As a result, I created a program, a spin-off of sorts of her program, called "Cocktails & Conversations." It is for women to have a safe place to come and let their hair down and be vulnerable through conversation. Things were going pretty well, and then my newfound attitude was tested. I received a call our brother was found unresponsive. Days later, he gained his wings.

My brother's death was a total wake-up call for me. I realized that my dad, mom, and brother had all died in their 60's. Sirens began to go off in my head. I thought, "I want to live beyond 60 and be around for my grandchildren." I looked at myself in the mirror and I was not happy with what

I saw. I was overweight at 355 pounds. I had not been taking proper care of myself. At that moment, I promised myself that I would change my life from the inside out and this time, when I smiled, it was going to be real. I have to admit, I had been here before. I had lost a large amount of weight before; I was even featured in a magazine. However, I did not want to lose weight that way, and I wanted it off fast.

I knew of several people who seemed to have had successful bariatric surgeries, so I had a consultation. On the drive home, I decided to call one of my good friends, because I know she would allow me to be vulnerable without judging me. With tears rolling down my face, I shared all of my pain associated with my weight and otherwise. After allowing me to have my private pity party, she suggested that I first try meal prepping before committing to surgery. The plan was for me to meal prep for at least a month, and if I did not see results, I could consider having bariatric weight loss surgery. Our conversation was uplifting, and I left feeling so encouraged. I immediately began carb cycling and walking. Two years later, I am 120 pounds lighter and maintaining my current weight. Although, I have not reached my goal weight, I am living a healthier lifestyle. With every step I take, I believe that I am closing the door on generational issues that have caused our family members not to live to see the age of 70. I know that God is not done with me yet. He is still molding me to be the woman He has predestined me to be. Is my life perfect? No. Am I learning how to handle the rough patches in the road better? Yes! It has taken me a long time to realize that unresolved issues will come back and wreck your life. You will take out your anger on a person that did not cause the pain. You will internalize everything, and your life will be on repeat. You and the people you love deserve the best version of you. Look around you. You are NOT stuck; decide today to make a choice, take a chance on yourself, make a needed change, and dare to stick it out. When I look back over my life, God shows me those moments that I thought I was alone, but he was there the whole time. My love languages are acts of kindness and affirmation. My daycare kids saved my life more times than I can count. No matter what was going on in my life, they made me feel loved and needed. The way they hugged me and smiled at me made me think that my life made a difference.

If you are reading this chapter, I can promise you two things. Tomorrow is not promised, and that there are more riches buried in cemeteries than any other place in the world because many of us are too afraid to live our dreams or our LIVES. It is time to LIVE! Below are some resources that were helpful for me during my lowest points. If you follow the call to action below daily, it will keep the barriers that you are working to break from forming again. I pray for your ever-lasting peace.

> *"Change is inevitable, but personal development is a choice."*
> **Bob Proctor**

Resources:

Bible Verses:

I can do all this through Him who gives me strength.

Philippians 4:13

Be strong and take heart, all you who hope in the LORD.

Psalms 31: 24

Other Resources:

National "You're Not Alone" Hotline: 1-800-273-8255

American Counseling Association – Grief and Loss Resources
https://www.counseling.org/knowledge-center/mental-health-resources/grief-and-loss-resources

Take Action!

For the next 30 days:

1. Write ten things that you are grateful for each morning.

2. Send a handwritten card out of the blue to 2 people a week.

3. Put sticky notes around the house in places that you can't miss them, affirming YOURSELF (ex. You are beautiful, You are amazing, etc.).

4. Go for a walk or march in place during commercials.

5. Buy the new lipstick or nail polish or thing that you want (within reason).

6. Find your "tribe" (a group that seeks to uplift others).

7. Volunteer at a shelter or someplace that serves others.

8. On the next page, write out the ten things that you love about yourself (you can do it).

Reflections

1. How can I incorporate these techniques into my life, so that I can create a legacy in my family and community?

_____

_____

_____

_____

2. How will I feel if I implement these things?

_____

_____

_____

_____

3. What barriers would keep me from obtaining the thing I am working towards?

_____

_____

_____

_____

4. Who do I know that can help me to move that barrier?

_____

_____

_____

5. What do I believe about myself & is it foundationally true?

_____

_____

_____

6. Where did my beliefs come from?

_____

_____

_____

7. What would happen If I changed how or what I thought about myself?

_____

_____

_____

_____

Meet Pamela

Pamela Alfred is a heart-lead Influencer; she is committed to advocating for women and children. She started her first home-based business, "Pamela's Playland of Learning", after receiving certifications for early childhood learning at Howard Community College. After relocating, she began a new career as an Executive, Assistant, later earning a certification in Billing & Coding through DeVry University. With a strong passion fueled by her own experiences, she launched "Cocktails & Conversations". A group where women can come and talk freely about life and the challenges that they face. She is a Mother, Grandmother, Sister, Woman of Faith, and a Friend to many.

Join Pamela in the Cocktails & Conversation Private Facebook Group.
https://www.facebook.com/pam.dorseyalfred

"Just when I think I have learned the way to live, life changes."

Hugh Prather

"To exist is to change, to change is to mature, to mature is to go on creating oneself endlessly."

Henri Bergson

7 Steps to Complete Peace!

Sharon Allen

I grew up in Baltimore in the mid 60's when life was full of the essentials of daily living. Family was considered the cornerstone of a good up-bringing, church was not a choice, and music was recorded on vinyl with an orchestra or band in the background. The hustle and bustle of trying to make ends meet was nowhere near as hard as it is today. I was considered one of the lucky ones though. I came from a two-parent household and what seemed to be a happy life. Little did most people know, I was more like Cinderella. Being plagued by the youngest-of-the-bunch syndrome set me up for some things that are still hard to talk about today. My story is nothing typical.

Unfortunately, I learned adult lessons way too early as a child; My first lessons in racism, colorism, and being bullied for anything you could name started in kindergarten. From the very fine and curly texture of my hair to me reading well, I was a target daily. Let's not talk about my very fair complexion. These few characteristics often led to lonely walks home in the afternoon. My place of refuge became the Enoch Pratt Free Library. I could go anywhere and do anything when I was there. Having a front row seat to different types of abuse, books were my escape from it all.

Six seemed to be my lucky number, that is how many books I was allowed to check out at one time. All I had were my books, music, and a collection of dolls that became my best friends.

The second lesson I learned was manipulation. As a people pleaser, I found myself trying to stay in the good graces of both of my parents and other people in my life. Making things worse, I was constantly compared to others as if I were not good enough just as I was. There is something about the way the things that are said to you as a child will stick to your very being as if it had been put in place with Gorilla glue. As a teenager, I tried hard to break away from the strict hand of correction at home, but it still followed me. After I started dating, I found myself with the same situation over and over again. I constantly felt like I did not quite measure up to everyone else's expectations of me. This followed me into adulthood and the cycle continued. I accepted things that were not in my best interest and overlooked other things for the sake of peace, while dying on the inside to a life I didn't want. Seems like one of the worst hands to be dealt, but I chose not to become a statistic.

After years of continuously being plagued by unwanted memories replaying in my head, those very memories propelled me into becoming self-sufficient and learning my purpose. I was then able to quiet the voices in my head making me believe I was not good enough. I achieved this by going to a counselor, as well as a life coach. They soon made me realize that I too was a child of God. As Psalm 139:14 NKJV states, I will praise You, for I am fearfully and wonderfully made. Marvelous are Your works. These affirmations helped me in many times of self-doubt back then and continues to help me today.

I have learned many valuable lessons in my life. I have learned about strength, tenacity, boldness, and patience through these processes. I have also learned to initiate my faith right away. Last, but not least, I have learned to give God my P.E.A.C.E.S! For me, that means:

Put

Everything and

All things

Completely in God's

Everlasting hands. Everyone has problems! I urge you to let Him lead you to your

Solutions!

These are my P.E.A.C.E.S.

PEACE 1

In 1998, I was a Physical Therapist Assistant. During the treatment of a combative patient with dementia, my last patient of the day, I suffered a life-changing injury while transferring him to the bed. This patient was what we called a "maximum assist" transfer. This requires at least two people to insure patient and staff safety. I went one step further and asked for a third person. During the transfer, the patient grabbed the chair and stopped the transfer midstream. Instead of the staff that was there using proper technique and body mechanics, both of my colleagues let the patient go. I was left holding all of the weight of the patient alone. This caused discs in my lower spine to shift. At that very moment, the pain became so intense that I could not be touched or moved. The pain shot from my back down through both hamstrings and they became numb, yet on fire, instantly! When I was finally able to move, I was rushed to the emergency room. I was placed in a room and left there alone for about an hour. No one helped me onto the bed or anything, so I had to manage this excruciating task by myself. Now I could no longer straighten out my left leg without intense pain. By then the pain had become ten times worse.

The doctor came in and I could tell something was not quite right. He began to speak to me with a certain tone. His tone and body language towards me indicated that he did not believe a word I was saying! The monster of racism once again reared its ugly head. I could not believe that someone who took an oath to help people was acting this way! Once the fiasco of taking X-rays, being given medication, and a bogus examination took place, I was free to leave. Since I was in no shape to drive, I called a friend to drive me home, which in itself was an ordeal of its own. After several attempts to get in the vehicle, I managed to drag myself onto the back seat where I laid the entire agonizing ride home. The pain medication I was given did not work to ease my pain at all. Needless to say, the ride home, getting out of the vehicle, and getting into the house into my bed was another lengthy feat. The next three months would prove to be a challenge. In the course of this time there were many doctor appointments, plenty of medications, and pain management, which did not take the pain away completely but made it manageable enough to return to work. At least that was what I thought. That injury sparked a whirlwind of brokenness and recovery from that moment on. Although I did not know it at that time, God certainly had more in store for me. Looking back, I realize that 7, the number of completion, has been the mold and outline of my life.

I hid not being able to use my leg from many people. I was able to manipulate my gait in such a way that it appeared that I was limping. I would do what we called in physical therapy "hiking my hip" to take a step with my left foot. I put on this facade for nearly six years, resulting in extensive nerve damage in my left foot and both legs. Going that long without treatment was not by choice. I went back and forth in court because Workers Compensation would not approve for me to have surgery. I got to the point where my legs felt like they were numb to touch, but on fire and cold at the same time. Then it happened -- I could no longer move my leg.

I learned that I had permanent nerve damage in both legs, from a momentary encounter with a combative patient. I could not bend my knee, move my foot up and down, wiggle my toes or anything! I not only lost the use of my left leg, but I also lost my career as well. In addition to that whirlwind, I also had several spinal surgeries, four to be exact. With these surgeries, I received rods, screws, and a cage at the base of my skeletal structure that prevented my spine from collapsing. I also had several fusions before it was all said and done. The first surgery was done through my stomach, which is known as an anterior approach. The other three were done through my back which is known as a posterior approach. Due to complications from the first surgery, I was hospitalized for thirteen days and had to have two blood transfusions. I had plenty of sleepless, painful nights and agonizing days in a turtle shell -- a hard, plastic brace fitted around my abdomen to prevent me from moving. BUT GOD!

In 2005 I went to physical therapy and worked diligently to regain use of my left leg. I received a vast assortment of physical therapy treatments, including range of motion exercises, electrical stimulation, strengthening and resistive exercises, deep tissue massage, ultrasound, aqua therapy, and transcutaneous electrical nerve stimulation (TENS) just to name a few. Seven years after my injury, I was up walking again!

PEACE 2

The journey to recovery was not an easy one. I had a few other complications along the way. This time, I was hospitalized for almost a week because I needed scar tissue removed from my spine. The scar tissue had wrapped around many nerves in my spine and caused pain and partial paralysis. During the scar tissue removal, my spinal cord was torn in three different areas. On top of that my right lung was not inflating properly. When I woke up in my room, I heard alarms and machines going off all around me, a signal that someone might be going into respiratory arrest, not realizing that someone was me! I was breathing so shallow that it did register on the machines. As a result of the torn spinal areas, I suffered what is called a spinal headache. The pain in my head was several times worse than a migraine. For several days, I laid in my hospital room in the dark with the television on with no sound. Even with this, the enemy could not keep me down, but he definitely gave me a hell of a sucker punch! That punch dazed me but did not knock me out. Ultimately, everything worked out and I returned home shortly after. Today I still have bouts with residual pain in my back and occasional nerve pain in my legs and feet. However, to God be the Glory! I am still walking!

Fast forward to 2012, 7 years after my first surgery, my husband left me; another whirlwind. I was on worker's compensation, but that ended two months after he left. I had no job or income and three children to take care of. Lord, what am I supposed to do now? The stress of figuring out the simple daily needs for my family as well as going through a divorce became overwhelming. There were many days that I did not want to get out of bed. However, my three precious gifts from God (my children) gave me strength to go on. I had to take a moment to remember who God created me to be. I am God-fearing, and survivor who is strong and courageous. I knew He already had a way mapped out for me. I had started a program for Sterile Processing and only had a few months left in school. I also had managed to save some money for a rainy day and received support from family and friends. I was able to provide for us for a while, so my stressors and fears were put to rest.

PEACE 3

It's 2013, now 7 years after my last surgery, I got a job as a Certified Registered Central Sterile Technician (CRCST). For those who don't know what that is, we are the ones who decontaminate, assemble, and sterilize the instrumentation and tools used for surgery. I cannot stress enough how grateful I felt. After years of unemployment, surgeries, and the possibility of being paralyzed hanging over my head coupled with a divorce and the mental strain that came with it all, I was drained. I went through highs and lows, but God never left my side. I felt alone often, but I knew HE was there. God blessed me with a great career and a wonderful team to work with.

"God's timing is always right!"
Sharon Allen

PEACE 4

Year 2020 marked a milestone in everyone's life. The Coronavirus (COVID-19) pandemic changed our world forever. I, like many, lost a loved one to this virus. I also know several people who have survived COVID-19. Working on the front line has been highly stressful and very overwhelming, to say the least. Through all of the darkness and sadness lurking around me, God shines a light every time we see a COVID-19 patient able to go back home with their family. Through yet another trial, GOD allowed me to reach my 7th year as a Central Sterile Tech.

PEACE 5

Year 2021 came in with celebration for me. It has been 7 years since my divorce. I never thought I would be here. I never thought that I could get through the loss of my home, my career, my marriage, and my health. Getting here was definitely a challenge, but "I can do ALL things through Christ who strengthens me." Phil. 4:13 NKJV. Since this year began, I started my own business, 7 PEACES, LLC. This is a place where women who have experienced any of life's challenges can come to network, share their joys and pains, and encourage one another daily, where they can expect to be uplifted, motivated, and rejuvenated.

PEACE 6

I co-authored and released my first book this year. You are reading it now (smile). I am expecting it to be a best seller because the women on this project are absolutely amazing! Each of them having a very astounding story of their own. Trauma has a way of affecting many people differently. Getting to the point of realizing that trauma may enter your life, but it does not have to rule your life was a major breakthrough for me. I was able to break many strongholds that held me back from being the person I was called to be. I found this breakthrough studying the Word, in counseling, and with a great support system. However, when the support is not present, I lean on daily affirmations like "I am great. I am worthy. I am Blessed." You get the point. I can now look forward to many new doors opening and opportunities coming my way. I thank God every day for opening my eyes to see His grace and mercy unfolding in my life. All I can say is, "If God is for us, who can be against us?" Romans 8:31 NKJV. Who would have thought I would be sharing my story? I hope to inspire women from all walks of life to keep striving.

PEACE 7

I lost my career, my marriage, and my house; yet through these life lessons, God saw fit to use me for HIS glory!!! I never thought I would survive any of this. In God's eyes, I must be pretty amazing. As the poem "*Recipe For An Amazing Woman*" goes...

Start with faith and honesty
Mix in pure humility
Add strength of character that rises above the stress of
life's surprises
Fold in personality
Toss with generosity
Pour in love from a heart that's true...
Yield: one TERRIFIC AMAZING YOU!!!

Author Unknown

Take Action!

What are 7 steps to bring you complete peace?

1. _____

_____

_____

2. _____

_____

_____

3. _____

_____

_____

4. _____

_____

_____

5. _____

_____

_____

6. _____

_____

_____

7. _____

_____

_____

Write several affirmations on index cards that will help you through your day. Post the affirmations in a place where you can read them daily. **Ultimately, the goal for this activity is for you find your PEACE!** Record a few of your favorites here.

_____

_____

_____

_____

_____

_____

_____

_____

_____

_____

_____

_____

_____

Reflections

1. How can I incorporate these techniques into my life, so that I can create a legacy in my family and community?

_____

_____

_____

_____

2. How will I feel if I implement these things?

_____

_____

_____

_____

3. What barriers would keep me from obtaining the thing I am working towards?

_____

_____

_____

_____

4. Who do I know that can help me to move that barrier?

_____

_____

_____

5. What do I believe about myself & is it foundationally true?

_____

_____

_____

6. Where did my beliefs come from?

_____

_____

_____

7. What would happen If I changed how or what I thought about myself?

_____

_____

_____

_____

Meet Sharon

Sharon Allen is currently a Certified Central Sterile Technician as well as a licensed nail technician. She has a background in Physical Therapy, Diagnostic Ultrasound, and as a Pharmacy Technician. She is also the founder and owner of 7 Peaces, LLC. This is a place where women who have experienced any of life's challenges can come and network, share their joys and pains, and encourage one another daily. At 7 Peaces, LLC, they can expect to be uplifted, motivated, and rejuvenated. We care, we share, and we are there! Let's grow together. Bring your PEACES: together we can make a whole!

You can contact Sharon here:
Email: sharons7peaces@gmail.com

Facebook Group:
https://www.facebook.com/groups/3615526861857387

> *"Self-knowledge is the beginning of self-improvement."*
>
> **Spanish Proverb**

"A humble knowledge of oneself is a surer road to God than a deep searching of the sciences."

Thomas A. Kempis

The Fog of My Identity: My Journey Through Depression

Hope Jackson

ave you every driven in fog? If you have then you know that your visibility is reduced, making it difficult to see things that are right in front of you. It could cause you to move off course due to the poor visibility, causing you to make bad decisions based not being able to see. I viewed my depression as fog. I could not see things that were right in front of me, and I made wrong turns in life, some which were harmful and unhealthy. I am going to take you on a journey through how I have navigated the fog of my depression and how I made my way to safety once the fog cleared. Have you ever allowed depression to rob you of what should be joyous moments in life?

> *Fear not, I am with you; be not dismayed, for I am your God; I will strengthen you, I will help you, I will uphold you with my righteous hand.*
>
> *Isaiah 41:10 ESV*

My early memories of depression began as a child around 8-9 years old. I remember always feeling sad and not understanding why. Even if I had a smile on my face, I still had this overwhelming feeling of sadness. I was afraid to tell anyone about my sadness because I did not want to create or cause any problems, so I just bottled it up inside wishing it would go away. The only problem with this was the older I got, the sadness got worse. I was withdrawn and did not hang out like most pre-teens since we could not afford outside activities. My great-grandmother made me participate in church activities, which was hard for me because I had to stand in front of people and recite poetry, dance, or sing with many friends, but most of my time was spent alone. Being alone was dangerous because in my alone time, I wished I were dead. I recall in elementary school, and even middle school, I complained about being sick even though I really was not sick. I just preferred to stay home versus being around other people. I never felt like I fit in with my family; I always felt different.

> *"Sometimes hope gets lost in a fog."*
> **Hope Jackson**

My first attempt to commit suicide was at 10 years old. I remember I was home alone and went to the kitchen to get a knife to cut my wrist and I did. My attempt was unsuccessful, but the thought never left my mind. I thought about how to end my life on many occasions. I did not feel like I could talk about what I was feeling because I did not feel like anyone would understand. I also did not really want to be burden to my mother. From what I could see she was struggling just to care for me, and my sister and I did not want my constant sadness and thoughts of dying to be another problem. Eventually my mother realized that something was wrong with me and got me into counseling. I did individual therapy and I talked about my family, my parent's divorce, the fact that I thought my sister hated me, and the fact that I did not feel like I belonged in my family. It helped but my sadness did not go away, it was still there. I never felt like belonged. I felt stupid, always struggling with schoolwork, and I was lucky to get C. I do not even recall ever making the honor roll. Eventually, I stopped going to counseling. Between middle and high schools, I cannot even count how many attempts or thoughts of suicide I had. Depression overpowered me to the point I had no confidence in myself and did not care how I looked. There were days I would not take a bath or shower, I was just this ugly, skinny, awkward teenager. Depression caused me to create these negative images of myself. These feelings and thoughts of myself carried on into my adult life, which eventually caused issues as I was began forming adult relationships.

> *For you formed my inward arts; you covered me in my mother's womb. I will praise You, for I am fearfully and wonderfully made.*
>
> *Psalm 139:13-14 NKJV*

There is no age limit on depression. If you are parent and have child that is always sad, withdrawn, or has no interest in social activities, understand they may be experiencing depression. Children carry stress and anxiety just as much as adults. Look to create a space to have open conversations with your kids.

Parenting and Depression

Being a parent is already a difficult job, being a single parent and battling depression makes the job even harder. I knew that prior to having kids that I was still struggling with depression, lack confidence, low self-esteem, and I truly had no intentions of having children. God had another plan for me.

I had my first daughter at 22 and the second at 23. Here I am, a statistic, a single mother of two children, no college education, and barely able to take care of myself emotionally and financially. If you are a mom, you know that after giving birth your hormones are all over the place and well that is an understatement. I was dealing with so much sadness, there were days I sat in the corner crying; some days I had no energy to get up and even take a shower. I went from depression to postpartum. My family stepped up because they saw me struggling so they helped me take care of my girls. This went on for 2 years, but my pride caused me to put on a fake smile to give them the illusion that everything was okay because I did not want to be a burden to them anymore.

> *"Place your oxygen mask over your nose before assisting others."*

As I got older, I still battled depression. I did not want anyone to see my sadness or my struggle so there were many nights that I would cry myself to sleep. I had planned my exit because the pain of living was too much to bear. I had created a will and written letters to each of the girls detailing my love for them. It was New Year's Eve Service, I had everything planned out to make it look like a car accident so that my life insurance would be paid out to the girls. God had a different plan because during the message, one of the words that was preached was about a broken plate beyond repair. The message in the word that God can heal brokenness, even we when we feel it is not able to be repaired. After that I had committed to myself and God. I no longer wanted to continue to live in the pain and I needed Him to heal me and fix my brokenness.

He heals the brokenhearted and binds up their wounds.

Psalm 147:3 NIV

The Healing

As mentioned above I had attended counseling, but it did not work for me. I realized it was not just about the counselor, it was also about me and my willingness to rid myself of the depression. I finally reached my breaking point. I was tired of being sad all the time. I was tired of life passing me by and I wanted to enjoy life. I decided to seek counseling again, but this time with the attitude of wanting to heal and begin to move forward. I realized that I had to treat counseling like weight loss; if you want to lose the weight, you have to put in the work, eat healthy, and workout. That is what I did with counseling; this time I put in the work and my counselor helped me to understand my depression. She taught me that I had to establish boundaries in my life and that it was not my responsibility to take care of everyone in my family. My primary responsibility was to take care of myself. It allowed me to be open and vulnerable with my counselors making them able to fully diagnose depression and PTSD, which was a result of childhood trauma, rape, loss, and domestic violence that I had experienced.

I was afraid to share because I was ashamed, so I tucked away and never really dealt with it. Once I recognized that I did not have to be ashamed, it was easier to be open and share with a trusted family member what had gone through. Once I started to release it all, I felt light. When I decided to begin the healing process, I realized that it would not be an overnight process; it is an ongoing process. I know that if I keep putting in the work and understand that I can still have moments of depression, it is more episodic and seasonal. Now I have the tools, resources, and a support system to help me to not sink back into the constant sadness and depression I used to feel.

For I know the plans I have for you, "declares the Lord," plans to prosper you and not to harm you, plans to give you hope and a future.

Jeremiah 29:11 NIV

God knew that I was going to battle with depression, which would obstruct my view of life and the plans that He had for me. I had to go through everything I went through in life, good and bad; God had a plan. I see the plans that He has for me, and that's why I started Always Hope. I share my journey with others and show others battling depression that you can heal, overcome, and be victorious.

I can admit that when I was writing my first book, *There Was Always Hope: Even When I Could Not See It*, I was nervous about putting my story out there, exposing myself and my truths. I was ready to submit my book to the publisher, but I had lost my job and shortly after I lost my home, leaving me homeless. All of this happened during the 2020 pandemic and it was a domino effect. Prior to really working on my healing, this would have caused me to sink into a deep depression, give up on myself, and have a whole pity party. Now I look to God and I started reciting this scripture.

> *Trust in Lord with all your heart and lean not on your own understanding; In all your ways submit to Him and will make your paths straight.*
>
> *Proverbs 3:5-7 NIV*

My first book was published in June 2020. I learned to manage my depression by recognizing that I am not in control of my life, only the way that I react. Understand that healing from depression is a journey, but if you are willing to put in the work, it is possible.

Things I learned as I navigated through my fog of depression.

1. **It is okay to admit that you are not okay**. For me I always felt like I needed to be the strong one in the family and to be there for everyone. I felt like everyone needed and depended on me. Therefore, I put my emotions and feelings aside. It took me years to take time to recognize how I felt and to admit that I do not always have to be the strong one. It is okay to admit that I was not okay and that it does not show weakness, but it shows your strength.

2. **Boundaries** – Set boundaries. "No" is a complete statement. I did not realize how much control I gave to others because I always said yes, to whatever it was they needed from me. In doing this, I left no time for myself. Even with my children, as they got older, I had to learn to set boundaries, not feeling that I had to be there to assist them with their issues. I had to teach them to figure things out for themselves.

3. **Professional Counseling** – I believe that God is a healer. I also believe in counseling. I have found a counselor who is a believer in Christ and has assisted with referencing the word in my healing process to overcome my depression and anxiety.

4. **Tasks** – Create task list of things you want to accomplish each day. This will help to keep your anxiety down as well show that you are accomplishing things every day.

5. **Accountability** – Get an accountability partner. Get someone that is truly going to hold you accountable and will really be there for you.

6. **Self-Care** – Make time for you. Monitor your food intake and exercise help to release those endorphins.

"New day begins in the darkest hour."

And God said, "Let there be light," and there was light.

Genesis 1:3

When we allow God into our dark times, he can reveal the light and give us a refresh. Here are 3 points.

1. God can heal what we reveal – we seek God and reveal to him the darkest parts of our life. He will provide the light we need to heal. Genesis 1:3-4

2. God is a God of order – learn to set boundaries, making God a priority. 1 Corinthians 14:33

3. Create room for God to work – God does is best work in us when we are dry and dark seasons of our lives. Genesis 1: 9-13

Take Action!

Have daily check-ins with yourself. Consider the following:

How to do feel today, emotionally, mentally and physically?

_____

_____

_____

_____

Am I setting proper boundaries?

_____

_____

_____

_____

Do I need to seek help from a professional Counselor?

_____

_____

_____

_____

What tasks must I complete today?

_____

_____

_____

_____

Have a checked in with my accountability partner?

_____

_____

_____

_____

What can I do today to take better care of myself?

_____

_____

_____

_____

Reflections

1. How can I incorporate these techniques into my life, so that I can create a legacy in my family and community?

_____

_____

_____

_____

2. How will I feel if I implement these things?

_____

_____

_____

_____

3. What barriers would keep me from obtaining the thing I am working towards?

_____

_____

_____

_____

4. Who do I know that can help me to move that barrier?

_____

_____

_____

5. What do I believe about myself & is it foundationally true?

_____

_____

_____

6. Where did my beliefs come from?

_____

_____

_____

7. What would happen If I changed how or what I thought about myself?

_____

_____

_____

_____

Meet Hope

Hope Jackson is a child of God, the founder of Always Hope, a published author, and a motivational speaker. She is also the co-host of Her Story Our Story. As a single mother, Hope experienced many of life's ups and downs and turned to God to help get her through whatever life threw at her. The grace and mercy God showed her during her trying times caused her to want to encourage and inspire others who are going through life's challenges. Her purpose is to motivate and encourage women to know that even in their darkest hours in life, there is Always Hope.

You can connect with Hope here:
Website: www.alwayshopellc.com
Instagram: _hopealways

"Trouble and perplexity drive me to prayer and prayer drives away perplexity and trouble."

Philipp Melanchthon

"Prayer is not an old woman's idle amusement. Properly understood and applied, it is the most potent instrument of action."

Mahatma Gandhi

Living on the Edge and Surviving the Drama

Katrina M. Fowlkes, RN, BSN

The beginning of my young, innocent life was a roller coaster. When I realized my father was never coming back, it was my fifth birthday party. I lived in Glenarden Apartments off of Brightseat Road in Landover, Maryland, where my mother later remarried. I was sexually molested within the first year of her involvement by my stepfather's sibling at six years old. A little later, I was raped by one of my mom's close friend's teenage sons at the age of eight and later I was abused by my mother, and others, because I look like the "Monk side of the family," resembling my father, the late Tony D. Monk. I was classified as the family's black sheep, or at least I felt that way; I was the only light-skinned kid. My mom and I had a complicated relationship because of her childhood and her marriage to my dad. My mom's drinking and me getting beaten because she saw my dad in my eyes was the story of my young struggling years. As a result, I thought I was worthless and deserved to be hurt.

I lived a dangerous life with no real guidance, hanging with those unsavory characters you would see committing the most heinous of crimes, until God blessed me with my first true love. My oldest son Kaylin Castle, weighing a full 2lbs and 11 oz, changed my life, my heart, and my career path. I did things my own, unorthodox way. Like having children and getting married after; you name it, I did it. I was told by multiple people that I would not amount to sugar-honey-ice-tea, if you know what I mean. But those very people gave me the drive to not become a statistic. At the young age of 23, I had my last son, Kai. Several years later, my doctor could not stop my uterus from an active bleed. Now, can you imagine if I had listened to every negative person putting me down every time I got pregnant? I would not be the mother I am today to four handsome young men (Kaylin, D'Artagnan, KyMauri, and Kai). Look at God and how he moves in every one of our lives.

I'm going to fast forward to 2020, during the pandemic of COVID-19. By far, 2020 was the most stressful year of my life; outside of my oldest son being shot coming out of a neighborhood store in Columbia, Maryland and my mother going into renal and congestive heart failure in 2019. Year 2020 claimed a total of seven family members' lives, two to COVID-19, except my mom, who decided to go into hospice, my area of expertise in my nursing career. My husband and I cared for my mom's every need until our Heavenly Father called her home with our entire family surrounding her.

Many of you are thinking, how on earth were you able to care for your mother after the horrible things that happened to you? It was nothing but the strength of my Heavenly Father, despite how my mom treated me and how my father was not there to protect me. They both were my first loves, and that bond would never die. God got a hold of my heart and allowed me to forgive them both. In fact, it was an honor to care for both my parents until the end of their lives.

The month of June was horrible for my family. After my mom died on June 5, 2020, my husband lost his mother two days later; my mom's sister died five days after her and my grandmother died on the 14th. Yes, the pain was indescribable. My family and I were walloped in 2020, as it would bring multiple people to their knees.

In late August, I was informed I had an abnormal tissue change in my right breast lymph nodes. A year and a half earlier, I was told I tested positive for CDH1, a breast cancer bracket the same as my mom. My mom had breast cancer in both her breasts, except her breast cancer went into her lymphatic system in 2016. I've had abnormal mammograms since June of 2018. Let's fast forward again. November 4, 2020, I had to have a radical double mastectomy. I was treated in the worse way possible by the very surgeon I entrusted my care to, all because I advocated for my life; the proof was in my pathology report. The left nipple was favorable for abnormal tissue growth. But, on January 07, 2019, this same surgeon told me I had a cyst, pain is not associated with breast cancer, and refused to biopsy the spot seen on my mammogram, MRI, and ultrasound. Oh, how horribly wrong she was; in fact, if I did not request to see an Oncologist and being placed on Chemo pills for a year and four months, I would probably be dead.

Back to my surgery, I was admitted for two days because of the vomiting and the horrific pain. The surgeon only gave me 15 pain pills upon discharge to last until my follow-up appointment that was scheduled 10 days out. The doctor refused to provide me with any pain coverage as if I was addicted to opioids. The breast surgeon did not cover my health care needs; but if my skin color was different, I know for a fact my care would have been upstanding. Behind the lack of care I received, my body suffered multiple complications; from extreme constipation, causing two bleeding ulcers to aspiration pneumonia with two collapsed lungs, the development of C-DIFF, Crohn's flare-up, and let's not forget the lymphedema that developed. Yes, you heard me! More than that, my left hip was broken and needed repairing and that is not even all. I had to handle yet two more deaths before and after my mastectomy; my uncle died in his sleep the week before my surgery, and on November 19th, my mom's baby sister died. The agony I felt when I could not see or touch my Aunt Carolyn brought me to my knees.

> *"God knows us better than we know ourselves because He created each of us; He never makes a mistake."*
> **Katrina M. Fowlkes**

When I came home from the hospital on January 1, 2021, another one of my mom's sisters died on the 2nd. All of this while trying to keep my head on right and be vital for my family. What should I do? LORD is all I can say!!! Lord, come down and take care of all of this hurt and pain for me, Lord. It was so hard to bear looking at myself as my breasts were now gone. "Why does my husband want to stay?" continuously ran through my mind. "I look like a man," I would scream out loud. God said to me in a soft voice; "I am right here with you. Go and take rest in me as I give you the desires of your heart."

As a teenager and going through all the hurt and pain, the Holy Spirit led me to read John 14 my entire senior year before I

> *"Let not your heart be troubled...*
> **John 14:1 (KJV)**

went to sleep. "Let not your heart be troubled, and neither let it be afraid, ringing through my soul..." God spoke to my heart and said, go back to the basics in my word. The gospel of peace, love, and healing; John 14 and 15. He also said, "get help. Get help! You are only one person." So, I did! I went to counseling because mental health is everything, and I got help.

God also moved me to start a family business to give back to our communities called Perfect Generation, LLC and Perfect Generation Ministries, a nonprofit. What a mighty God we serve. God also had me look at the positive things that have happened to me despite the horror show that has been displayed in my life. The birth of two beautiful grandbabies Alaya Castle and D'Artagnan Benjamin Jr., not to mention my oldest grandson Christopher by way of my beautiful daughter Boogie. He had me see that He has surrounded me with love from my husband Damon, my sons

KyMauri, Kai, D'Artagnan Sr., and Kaylin. But, significantly, my special daughter Jazmia, by way of my son Mauri, has taken care of my every need while she continued her education as an honor student. What love I have immediately surrounded me!

God also said, "What about your sisters who pray for you and encourage you daily?" Yes, I would be lost if I did not have my sisters, and you definitely know who you are. My Black Queens and prayer warriors. "Oh, you cannot forget your Godparents Lee and Butch, who have been there every step of the way since you were twelve years old. Let's not forget your other mothers in Norfolk and Mississippi. What about your church family, especially those who really know who you are without judging you? Child, do you know how rich you are?" is what the Lord told me. "You are so blinded by the bad things you cannot see the blessings around you. Yes, your earthly father and mother are gone, but you still have fathers and mothers around you to love on you like your father-in-law, your sister-in-law, your family from both sides. Most importantly," God said, "You have Me because I will never forsake you nor leave you."

> "...I will never leave thee, nor forsake thee
> **Hebrews 13:5 (KJV)**

That alone gave me the strength to hold on and let go of the many toxic things in my life; horrible friendships, negatively thinking about myself, cursing like a sailor, not going to God with my hurt, taking care of myself last, not listening to my loved ones, not believing in myself, not trusting God, reacting negatively, and not loving myself. I want to encourage each person reading this to allow the Lord into your life. Trust that your journey called life is not for you. It's actually for the people God will send to you to help them through their trials. Remember this, God knows us better than we know ourselves because He created each of us; He never makes a mistake.

Reflections

1. How can I incorporate these techniques into my life, so that I can create a legacy in my family and community?

_____

_____

_____

_____

2. How will I feel if I implement these things?

_____

_____

_____

_____

3. What barriers would keep me from obtaining the thing I am working towards?

_____

_____

_____

_____

4. Who do I know that can help me to move that barrier?

_____

_____

_____

5. What do I believe about myself & is it foundationally true?

_____

_____

_____

6. Where did my beliefs come from?

_____

_____

_____

7. What would happen If I changed how or what I thought about myself?

_____

_____

_____

_____

Meet Katrina

My name is Katrina M. Fowlkes. I am a wife to an amazing King, Damon and I am the mother of four outstanding young Kings and two beautiful young Queens. God has blessed me to be a grandmother of two handsome princes and a beautiful princess. I have a career as a Registered Nurse working towards my Nurse Practitioner degree with a focus in Family Practice. I am the owner of Perfect Generation, LLC, and Perfect Generation Ministries, a nonprofit business launching in April 2021. I am an advocate for women, especially minority women, who struggle with the world on their backs. I am overjoyed to be a part of this intoxicating opportunity as a co-author of "Her Story Our Story." Stay encouraged and safe. This portion of the book is dedicated to my family, friends, all the women hurting and striving for better, and breast cancer survivors; especially, my mom the late Patricia M. Hopkins. Despite the ups and downs of our relationship. I have learned so much from my beautiful mother; like never giving up! Be Blessed and stay in God's Word.

"Without wearing any mask we are conscious of, we have a special face for each friend."

Oliver Wendell Holmes

"One who's our friend is fond of us; one who's fond of us isn't necessarily our friend."

John Hay

I Will Lay Down But Never Bow Down

Saprina Allison, RN

Hello Morning rain it's so nice to see you
I have to remember even in a storm to be grateful
Some will look and wish your clouds to just go
Me, I will focus on finding your rainbow
Every storm in life you might not have the answer to
If you hang in there long enough, the sun will shine through
None of us have waiting for a catastrophe in life on our bucket list of things to do
It's not what happens to us but how and what we respond to
So, shoulders back, head up because that's what champions do
Yes, before you ask, I see a Champion in you!

By: Saprina Allison

The weekend of November 5-6, 2016 was a weekend to remember. It was full of surprises, history making moments and a celebration to match. With tickets for the football game on Sunday in hand, driving from Virginia a day earlier was supposed to be for leisure and shopping. However, Saturday turned into an extra special day. I surprised my dear friend who was celebrating her promotion to Lieutenant as a police officer and that was a big deal. After celebrating half the night away, I was ready for some football. As fate would have it, the trash talking and banter started in the parking lot. The closer I got to the stadium the air became thick enough to cut with a knife. Everywhere you looked, someone was yelling with purple pride or swinging a terrible towel and yes, I was ready for the shenanigans.

My team came out like they always do, ready to play smash mouth football and ran the first touch down into the end zone where I was sitting. The rest of the game pretty much went the same way for the remaining three quarters. One important detail that was left out, I had a four-hour ride home with one of the biggest Pittsburgh fans ever.

Monday morning greeted me with a 9 AM appointment with my family nurse practitioner for my annual physical. Needless to say, cloud nine became my dance floor because everything went well. Waking up the next morning, I noticed my temples tapping mildly. This was a familiar feeling and at that time medicine wasn't required. Little did I know that mild tap would later be referred to as the beginning of the end.

Continuing to ignore what was happening, getting to work became the priority instead of me. As far back as age 7, headaches and blurry vision was something that I lived with. Ignoring these symptoms was a huge mistake and this allowed the invisible monster living on the inside to go undetected. Functioning in pain was like putting on my shoes every day. Besides, several women in my family suffered from migraines so it was considered what we call a family trait. This nagging situation went on for days with the intensity increasing. I did not seek medical attention because it was easier to blame it on stress and so as usual, I continued to march on.

Being a nurse full time, a mother of two sons with my oldest son being deployed at that time and my youngest son a high school basketball player with a college decision to make, my life did not lack stress. Getting sick was not an option for me, at least that was the lie I told myself. It is important to stop and listen when your body is trying to tell you something. As the old saying goes, people don't cry for nothing. Well, your body does not hurt for nothing. Pain is a warning sign of what's to come if it's not treated.

> *"Your body does not hurt for nothing. Pain is a warning sign of what's to come if it's not treated."*
> **Saprina Allison**

Thinking back on it, there was something different about this headache. It never went away. My head felt as if a sharp, hot knife was cutting through it, while having a root canal with no anesthesia in the middle of the North Pole in minus 16-degree weather. Imagine that. As my favorite day of the week was approaching, this headache was becoming a real nag. Thursday came and it felt like the three previous days. That was my normal hair day but not this time. I had just enough strength to make it home and fall in bed. There is a first time for everything, and this was the first I had ever canceled a hair appointment.

Arriving to work late on Friday, the lights were so bright that keeping my sunshades on in the building was necessary. Due to the pressure increasing in my eyes I could only see shadows. The very sound of the bell from the elevator seemed 10 times louder than normal. I made a B-line to my desk hoping that sitting still would calm this beast in my head. Within minutes of me sitting down, life as I knew it was over. I had a seizure for more than six minutes. Unfortunately, seizures cause a lack of oxygen to the brain and can leave some people with brain damage. It was a good thing I worked with nurses because the response to the call for help was swift. I don't remember too much after that until I woke up.

I woke up to hearing pure pandemonium in the background. As if I was on a tropical island with blue water, a Jamaican accent was the first thing I recognized. The other voices were loud sounding as if it was a Saturday night house party, and somebody cheated in the spades game. Figuring out that the commotion being made was about me, I tried my best to pull myself together. Then, out of nowhere a voice screaming as if a flood was coming to take over the land, this New York accent was familiar and could only be one person. Screaming as loud as she could, "Open your phone, I need to call home for you!"

At this point I was wishing the floor would just open up and swallow me. Still not realizing the magnitude of what happened, the ambulance arrived. That's when it became apparent something was really wrong. It is one thing to walk into work not feeling well and leave for the day on your own but to walk in and be rolled out on a stretcher was a gut punch. Rather than give into what I was really feeling, I put my lipstick on, sunshades too and decided to wave at the crowd as I left the office. Holding it together until getting into the ambulance was hard but I did it. Hearing those ambulance doors close was like hearing the steel bars of a maximum-security prison door slam. I was locked into this situation with no escape.

Every thought imaginable during that short ride to the hospital crammed itself into my brain. I wondered if I had put the right village in place for my sons, did I invest enough in my retirement should anything happen to me and last, but not least, would they miss me as much as I would miss them. The thought of not seeing my God-daughters' sweet round face was the ultimate. The water works started. Feeling helpless, it was only one thing I knew to do. My conversation with God started like this, *Father, you said that in the time of trouble that you would hide me in your secret tabernacle, I need you to hide me. I activated my faith immediately.*

The ambulance pulled up to the hospital and the doors swung open. The first thing I noticed was a man, slender build with a baseball cap, standing in front of the ER with his hands in his pockets. As I was being taken out of the ambulance, he walked over to the stretcher and softly whispered I am here now, you will be just fine. Then a soft gentle kiss was planted in the middle of my forehead and off into the hospital the stretcher rolled.

Having to call family was no fun at all. I was worried most about my grandmother. My mother had just passed away three years prior, so hearing that I was sick would have not been good. Keeping that in mind, the next best option was my aunt. The next phone call was my anchors, my cousin in Florida and my girlfriend in Maryland. As usual, my cousin held a straight face with a calm voice and was strong. Later, I found out that was a front. My girlfriend in Maryland truly couldn't understand what was happening because we had spent the weekend together. Trying to understand anything she was saying was almost impossible. She was talking way too fast and curt but. "Do I need to come there?" came out clear. At that time there was no need for anyone to come because the puzzle was still being put together.

While lying in the hospital, I made up my mind that no matter what the doctor told me a smile would be my reaction. Yes, I was laying down, but I wasn't going to bow to anything. Your attitude determines your altitude. I was clueless about the beast living on the inside of me that was causing all the drama, but I knew the God I served. Every test possible was done and nothing

> *"Yes, I was laying down, but I wasn't going to bow to anything."*
> **Saprina Allison**

showed up. Baffled by the results, this was the beginning of my journey as a patient.

After leaving the hospital, things were so uncertain. It was apparent that the news had spread throughout my office. A ton of phone calls, text messages and cards spoke volumes. By this time my grandmother found out, she called my uncle in Michigan and they were Virginia bound. I felt bad because one of my friends was so traumatized from the incident, all she remembers is crying and calling another friend. It's always one friend that will get you together and that phone call came with specific instructions. Then reality hit like a ton of bricks. My driving privileges had been revoked, I had to see a specialist, and like rapid fire appointment after appointment to run more tests. At every appointment it seemed as if another pill was added to my medication list. By the way, the medication that worked for me my insurance company no longer paid for. Trying to find a medication that worked made me even sicker than I was before.

Frustrated with the process of regaining my health, periodically I would still hear a voice accompanied by a kiss in the middle of my forehead saying, "It's fine you will be ok." Calls would still come from family members just to check in on me. Without realizing it, I started getting the same phone call every Wednesday and Thursday.

The Wednesday phone call was short, sweet and to the point. "Hey Girl, how is my sister? Don't talk. I just wanted you to know I love you."

The Thursday call was a little different, it was two questions. Are you resting? Do I need to come over there to get you together? Followed by, "Because you know I will." Before an answer could be given, the phone would hang up.

Suddenly, things took a turn for the worst. The aftereffects of the seizure and wrong medicine began, starting with episodes of short-term memory loss, hair loss, and I developed a stutter. These things made me self-conscious and depressed to say the least. This was a type of darkness that was on TV, not in real life. Keeping true to my word, I still smiled through the tears. At this point laying down or falling down was happening frequently, but I still didn't bow down. After a year of trial and error, the request for an MRI was met with hesitation. Finding out what was wrong with me was consuming my life. Something was there but it just didn't have a name. Sounding like the old AOL dial up internet service I heard, "You have Chiari Malformation."

My response was, "I have a Darien and a Gary. I don't have a Chiari."

So, to put this in layman's terms, I was born with the bottom part of my brain pushing down out of my skull. This disorder is treatable but not curable. Some people are treated with medications while others have to have brain surgery. So much of my life made sense after talking to the doctor but it didn't make sense. All of the aches and pains that plagued me and I thought was just nothing was really something. Again, listen to your body, it gives warning signs. What I thought was that the family trait of migraines was not just a migraine, it was a Chiari headache. The blurry vision did not come from sitting in front of the TV too close. The back and neck pain were not from me being overactive or lifting a heavy patient. I had a major medical diagnosis that was masking itself as other things. At home crying, I heard that voice again say, "You will be just fine."

For a moment, I forgot who I was, but the reminders came very quick. I shut down and was knocked down, but I didn't bow down to this disorder. For some reason my phone would not stop ringing this particular day. The first phone call I heard a voice say, "Ma, God gives his toughest battles to his strongest soldiers."

The next message was, "Sugar Dumpling, I am calling to check on you, just remember whose you are."

The third message was simply, "Ma, I love you."

It is imperative to surround yourself with those who will remind you to stand anyway and when you can't stand on your own, they will become your anchors. My mind shifted and so did my life. The acronym A.A.C.T became not just something to say but something to do.

Activate Your Faith

Advocate For Self

Create a new Life Plan

Treat each day like you don't have time to waste

Daily affirmations and keeping my faith intact went with me to my next doctor's appointment and each one after that. I intentionally got up every day and no matter what, put my pearls and lip-gloss on because I didn't have to look like what I was going through. Getting back to my old self, my hairstylist would make time for me and let's not talk about my nail tech. If she had to make a house call, it was not a problem. In her words, you don't have to do this alone. I made sure that my medical team was on the same page as I was. Advocating for self was an essential part of my recovery. When I would get some push back from my medical team, I pushed back. The word "no" was not an option, and I often reminded my doctor of my goals, not hers. Who says that I can't do anything? Yes, I can, it will just be done a different way, but it will get done. The only choice for me was to live my life, not my diagnosis. My mother named me Saprina, not Chiari. Is every day a good day physically? No, it's not, but everyone has physical challenges from time to time. Every day we have to make the conscious decision and be intentional in our actions.

After going through what I called the pit of hell, educating myself and others around me became not only a priority but my mission. After being a nurse for 22 years, I was diagnosed with something rare. Something that I had never heard of and a lot of doctors were not familiar with treating. Telling people what I was diagnosed with was like a knock-knock joke.

Knock! Knock! Who's there?

Chiari Malformation.

Who? What type of formation?

So, I started talking to anyone that would listen. Reading every bit of information, I could get my hands on and asking questions often to gain clarity was becoming second nature. The more I talked with others, not only did I find out how broken our medical system was for some getting treatment but the care being received by some was lackluster at best. This fueled me even more, I started to find out that people with this disorder were labeled as medication seekers and frequent flyers. People were suffering and left to their own devices to figure out this complicated disease on their own. As a nurse, it was heartbreaking to see but as a patient, I knew what had to be done. I created a new life plan for myself and begin to share it with others to empower them.

After getting the medication that I needed, life started over for me. My tribe continuously encouraged me through prayer until I was standing strong again. Now I am back and better than ever. Always remembering that I might lay down, get knocked down, even shut down for a brief moment but I will never bow down to anything! I don't live with Chiari Malformation; it lives with me. God calls the shots, not my disorder. Exercising when I can, making a conscious effort to eat well, resting and keeping my attitude in check is all in a day's work. Every day my goal is to be a living example to those with invisible pain or a chronic disorder that there is life after your diagnosis. I truly do treat every day like I don't have time to waste because I don't. There are lives that have been divinely assigned for me to touch. Existing but not living will keep others bound and held hostage by this and other disorders. Yes, I still face some challenges but I A.A.C.T like I know and climb the mountain that has been assigned to me. Then I stand on the top of it. Always remember to lay down to get rejuvenated but never bow down.

> *But they that wait upon the Lord shall renew their strength; they shall mount up with wings as eagles; they shall run, and not be weary; and they shall walk, and not faint.*
> **Isaiah 40:31**

SisterGirl
By: Saprina Allison

Sister, stop thinking that showing your strength means
saying, "I will take care of everybody else first and then
me."
You know staying so busy until it's hard for you to breathe
Schedule packed tight with a whole lot of fun things to do
Only problem is, ain't none of it for you!
A big smile, huge personality, and brilliance is all a part of
your evolution.
To every question asked... You are the solution
Controlling the room without even having to speak
His fresh anointing flowing from the crown of your head to
the sole of your feet
Did God really mean for you to have all of those business
ideas?
Look in that toolbox; everything is there accept fear
It's time to come out of hiding and off of the back shelf
Don't wait any longer; unwrap the gift that's on the inside
AND FREE YOURSELF
Affirm, daily, something powerful about you
I know when I open my eyes... I SHAKE HELL LOOSE

Take Action!

How will you A.A.C.T today?

Activate Your Faith

_____

_____

_____

Advocate for Self

_____

_____

_____

Create a new Life Plan

_____

_____

_____

Treat Each Day Like You Don't Have Time to Waste

_____

_____

_____

Reflections

1. How can I incorporate these techniques into my life, so that I can create a legacy in my family and community?

_____

_____

_____

_____

2. How will I feel if I implement these things?

_____

_____

_____

_____

3. What barriers would keep me from obtaining the thing I am working towards?

_____

_____

_____

_____

4. Who do I know that can help me to move that barrier?

_____

_____

_____

5. What do I believe about myself & is it foundationally true?

_____

_____

_____

6. Where did my beliefs come from?

_____

_____

_____

7. What would happen If I changed how or what I thought about myself?

_____

_____

_____

_____

_____

Meet Saprina

After 22 years of being a nurse Saprina was diagnosed with an incurable but treatable brain disorder called Chiari Malformation. Saprina decided without apology to LIVE HER DREAMS NOT HER DIAGNOSIS!

Being gifted to bring words to life through poetry and storytelling, Saprina intentionally finds creative ways to assist others diagnosed with invisible pain or a chronic disorder to find their YES! Not only does she teach those with Chronic Disorders how to create a new life plan, Saprina is an example of how to get it done. A mother, Nurse, Poet and Radio Personality she is truly living her dreams.

Combining poetry with her Acronym A.A.C.T (**A**ctivate your faith, **A**dvocate for self, **C**reate a new life plan and **T**reat each day like there is no time to waste) lives are changed daily.

HER MANTRA IS: RUN HARD DREAM BIG CREATE A LEGACY

"*Power does not corrupt. Fear corrupts, perhaps the fear of a loss of power.*"

John Steinbeck

Embrace My Truth

Sasha E. Butler

My greatest fear is not that I am dying, nor am I worried that people will soon forget about me. As I sit here reflecting on my life and how much time I wasted rationalizing and intellectualizing everything, I cannot help but wonder: why is my life such a struggle? All I ever dreamt about was making a difference in the lives of others. People always tell me, "Girl, you are so brilliant!" Yet, I constantly battled against insecurity and doubt, which has become like cancer and has robbed me of decades of a healthy and fulfilling life. I wasted so much time and energy searching for the meaning of life. I have gambled away or sold everything, including my self-respect, for that 'one thing' that could change everything. I used to think that the 'one thing' was making more money because the overwhelming fear of poverty held a tight grip on me. It was like the invisible boogeyman that kept me in a state of panic, constantly feeling ashamed and inadequate. I thought maybe an intimate partnership or business relationship could help solve my problems. Still, those things seemed only to perpetuate the fears that haunted me and held me back from my most authentic self.

I secretly lived a life of negative, self-fulfilling prophecies. The only thing that helped me was my gift for inspiring people. I have a natural ability to work a room, ignite it with confidence, and motivate people to act on their dreams. However, I could not finesse myself into believing that I belonged in that room. This self-doubt plaguing me was not really about a lack of confidence. I was convinced of the greatness in me at the age of three. The doubt that made me feel like a misfit: was summed up in dollars and cents. Poverty is my greatest fear. I expended so much of my energy and resources trying to distance myself from it, but it seemed determined to stick closer to me than a friend.

Whenever an opportunity presented itself, I seized it with confidence, but it would eventually slip from grasp. I could not sustain the belief that something extraordinary was happening for me. I was always in conflict with my dreams and my reality. I fully believed in my dreams, but poverty and a lack of pedigree had a spell over me. I perfected my gift and walked in my greatness while questioning where I fit in. I never discovered that 'one thing' that had the power to transform my narrative. Instead, I became addicted to pursuing people, places, and things to deal with the trauma my poverty mentality had inflicted on me as an adult. As I stand here looking back on what my life should have been or could have been, I am afraid my life will be in vain – meaningless, pointless, a series of what-ifs, but never fully fulling my purpose. It is this fear that places me at a crossroad. I know I must die to the broken and limited version of me and embrace my truth.

My Journey

I was born in the Bronx, New York. My mother raised me, my two older sisters, and my older brother in the now-infamous Edenwald Projects until I turned eleven. As a young girl, I struggled to make the right choices and to allow my Christian upbringing to lead me in the right direction. I enjoyed engaging in intellectual conversations in Sunday School and Bible Study, and I loved God, but not so much church folk. I never felt like I fit in because I was not part of the click. I filled my void of not feeling like I belonged with reckless behavior. My poor decisions should have lost me my freedom and cost me my life. However, no matter how far I strayed, God protected me. I also attribute my survival to having a praying great-grandmother and mother who instilled in me the 'Power of a Dream.' My mother, a retired teacher/principal, reminded me of my destiny to do great things in this world one day. She has always been my greatest cheerleader.

Although we did not have a lot of money, she exposed us to Broadway shows, opera, and museums. She introduced me to African culture and the richness of my Black heritage. We took trips to the library to check out literature written by poets and authors from the Harlem Renaissance period, including Claude Brown, Richard Wright, James Baldwin, Langston Hughes, and Zora Neale Hurston. Two books influenced my interest in social justice: "Manchild in the Promised Land" by Claude Brown and "Black Boy" by Richard Wright. My favorite poem, "Dreams," was written by poet Langston Hughes:

Hold fast to dreams, for if dreams die, life is a broken-winged bird that cannot fly. Hold fast to dreams, for when dreams go, life is a barren field frozen with snow.

Poems and passages like these inspired me to keep dreaming despite the adversity I faced. Reading and writing poetry motivated me to take on leadership roles and become active in my community.

My passion for helping people never waned because of my insecurities. The written and spoken word is the vehicle that activates my gift for inspiring people from all walks of life. I love helping people overcome their insecurities, even though I used to cling to mine like a security blanket. In high school, I could encourage my teammates on the track team to believe they could win the race even when the odds were against them. In college, I was elected president of the Black Student Union. It was a role that defined much of my future endeavors. I excelled in my role as a leader because it was one of the few times in my life when I did not worry about poverty.

Serving as a leader in college helped me realize that I needed to use my gift to empower young people. Many of my peers struggled to see their value and purpose in a predominantly white college. I was passionate about helping them overcome a limiting mindset that convinced them their skin color somehow disqualified them from achieving great things in life. I did not fully understand the irony of being insecure and a person of influence at the same time. It would take years for me to overcome my insecurities. I had a lot of growing to do to see my value despite my limitations. I needed to learn how to embrace my truth. In my senior year, I was selected to deliver the baccalaureate speech at my alma mater, Manhattanville College. My speech was an encouraging message about following your dreams and pursuing the career you loved. As much as I agreed with those sentiments, I had already decided that making lots of money was my only goal.

Once I began my job hunt, I learned quickly that a degree in English Literature and Writing was not in demand. I bounced around between temp agencies before my friend's father at a technology company intervened and helped me get a job in his company. My degree did not open the door to the income I had expected. I started at the bottom. At the time, it felt like the sting of poverty all over again. I worked my way up slowly but never made a salary I thought matched my talent. After eight years, a friend of mine left the company for a lucrative position at a large New York City company. He recommended me, and I received an interview. Getting an interview was never easy, but acing an interview was something I did consistently. The company offered me seventeen thousand dollars above my previous salary at the last company. I had access to a company credit card and car service to take me home. I also stayed at villas during business trips and enjoyed an expense account.

I was finally making the type of money I envisioned. I had a nice apartment in a safe neighborhood, a new car, I paid my bills in full and on time, and I had money left to save and invest. I conquered poverty, but I discovered I was still miserable. Whenever I ordered a car service to take me home, I slept peacefully during the forty-minute ride up the

West Side highway. After a few months, I could no longer sleep because I felt empty and depressed. I realized poverty was not the issue; I was the culprit. For so long, I blamed my lack of contentment on external factors. Now I was faced with the reality that I alone was causing myself so much anxiety. It was an awakening – the beginning of my journey to embracing my truth.

The Awakening

I hoped by leaving American Express and applying for a job at my previous company, I would solve my problem. Again, I aced the interview. Prodigy was comfortable because it was familiar and my first real job out of college. The company offered me more money, and I was closer to home. The euphoria of the reunion only lasted a few months. Six months later, the company downsized my department, and I was laid off. Walking toward the outsourcing center, the fear of poverty tried creeping back into my mind. I felt like I was in the Twilight Zone as I sat in the conference room waiting to speak to the recruiter hired to help me find a new job. I remember him telling me that I could write my ticket because of my knowledge and years in the industry. Most people who lost their job quickly found a job at other companies and made twice their salary.

Almost everything the recruiter was saying to me was a blur. I recall him asking me what he could do for me and how much money I wanted to make. He had a whole list of companies ready to hire me. It was in that moment something awakened in me. The recruiter was shocked when I responded, "Nothing!" I was convinced there was no amount of money or job he could offer me that would change my narrative. I knew I needed to change my perspective on life and open my mind to its possibilities rather than its limitations. I thanked him for his time and left there with no prospect of employment. I was no longer afraid because I was ready to embrace my truth. I finally understood I could not overcome poverty by chasing money. Prosperity can manifest once I decided to pursue my purpose.

Realities of Faith

When I walked out of that door of the recruiter's office, a new door into my journey opened. I left full of faith, joy, and confidence because I was on the road to living in my purpose. I was about to venture out into deep uncharted territories that would challenge and build up my faith. I had not anticipated that my path toward my purpose would be a difficult road ahead of me. The next ten years would be a series of starts and stops, successes and failures. Doors of opportunity opened for me, only to shut because of circumstances beyond my control. Consulting contracts would evaporate before I signed on the dotted line. Grants once approved were now being denied. I fought a vicious battle against discouragement and depression threatening to defeat me.

The obstacles in my way felt like they were going to consume and break me. There were days when I found it difficult to see the sunshine through the rain because I was in such great pain. I knew commitment and consistency were roads I had to walk alone. I found comfort in a quote by Charles Haddon Spurgeon, "The strong are not always vigorous, the wise not always ready, the brave not always courageous, and the joyous not always happy." His words inspired me to surround myself with people who understood this journey and were willing to share their stories and give excellent advice. I learned so many lessons during this season. The most important one is the difference between success and fame. The Collins dictionary defines fame as "the state of being widely known or recognized; renown; celebrity." Success is "the favorable outcome of something attempted." The fact that I did not give up and I was fully embracing my truth meant I had already succeeded!

Embrace My Truth

I was searching in all the wrong places for something already embedded in me. My thirst for 'something' greater required me to correct the cracks in my character. The belonging that dodged me all these years was right in front of me. I just needed to spend more time looking in the mirror. Embracing all my truth inspired me because going through the process helped me realize I am a valuable piece of God's master plan. He created and crafted me to be that one-of-a-kind 'one thing' the world needs. My journey, with its ups and downs, became a blueprint for overcoming adversity and defeat. My story is not an accident but an antidote for brokenness and hopelessness.

A survivor of an abusive marriage, a failed business, and abandoned friendships are not just stories about the trauma I endured; they embody messages of hope and forgiveness, reconciliation, and resilience. I am the sum of all my experiences, yesterday and today. It is on me to choose if I am going to give up or get up. My experiences made me who I am. My struggles have become my greatest assets and my tools for success. They inspire and help people discover their purpose. My passion and my prosperity are rooted in developing and empowering people in my sphere of influence. I prosper when they learn how to embrace their truth!

The Goal

My story is an instrument designed to ignite your journey. It does not end with an awakening because the journey never ends; it always begins. My message to you is to stop running away from you and start running in the direction of your dreams. The good and the bad, all of it is you! The key is perspective and how you leverage your narrative. We are all designed to prosper, but never exchange your integrity for currency. The value of your character will always be worth more than what you have in the bank.

People will never fully understand the cost of what it took for you to get where you are today. Whether you are standing on a stage speaking to millions of people or just doing home videos to start, you paid the price to be authentically you. Gospel singer CeCe Winans calls it the oil in your alabaster box. Your oil is priceless because it is the essence of who you were when you were born, who you are today, and who you will be in the future. The only way to protect your oil is to embrace your truth. The pain, the stains of shame, and the victory you claim are all of you. The goal is to stay connected with the greatness not only in you but the greatness that is you.

The Value of Growth

The keys to success are born of great sacrifice. We live in a society that defines a person as either a winner or loser - a giver or taker. The challenge other people try to force us to make is choosing either our principles or our career. To have both, I had to step out outside of my comfort zone. Perfecting my craft is the superpower that made it possible for me to live my convictions and pursue my dreams. You must be willing to step outside your comfort zone to learn something new continually. In the unknown realm, inventions are born, books are written, and solutions to problems are discovered. If you do not grow, you will sell your principles for a price. Growth is not accidental, but it must be intentional.

In the 15 Invaluable Laws of Growth, John Maxwell said, "Once you're done with your formal education, you must take complete ownership of the growth process" for the rest of your life. It is not others' responsibility to guarantee your personal and professional growth or even your spiritual well-being. The decisions you make today to grow will impact your success tomorrow. It is up to you to cultivate an atmosphere of excellence and consistency where your dreams can develop and grow. Allow your faith to be stretched and your convictions challenged. If you keep going and keep growing, you will discover your full potential.

Love What You Do

We are all destined for something greater than ourselves. Are you wondering if what you currently do is right for you? If you answered yes to this question, you probably have not discovered what it is that you genuinely love. When you find it, you know it! Collaborating with individuals and organizations to equip leaders locally and globally is what I love to do. If you are still searching, I encourage you to keep inquiring and exploring. Look for opportunities to serve. Never discount the things you do for free, especially if they bring you joy. I love to do community service and work with youth to help them become globally competent. I invest time motivating them to use their voice for social change and to work together with their peers in other countries to share ideas and discover solutions to real-world problems. The things I love and did for free now bring in income.

The things you do without getting paid are usually the key to your purpose and sustainable income. Think outside the box. Even if your imagination tells you it is impossible, let your heart guide you to the possibilities. I always look for connections when I meet people. Their profession and background do not matter; I am confident my Divine design helps individuals become better at what they do and who they are. Do not judge your potential by the size of your paycheck or allow your position in life determine your eligibility for success. Once you discover and embrace that 'one thing' designed for you, it will ignite a fire in you and create a path for you. Perfect it, and nothing or no one can stop you from being successful.

Create Your Legacy

We are the product of those who have influenced us both directly and indirectly. Some people serve as our mentors, while others are authors and speakers we admire. We cannot fully embrace our truth without recognizing and celebrating those who have profoundly impacted our lives. Our treasures lie within our encounters with family and friends and people we meet throughout our life. Creating a legacy is not limited to famous people. Everyone's calling is to make a difference in the lives of others. Jim Rohn, a motivational speaker, said, "All good men and women must take responsibility to create legacies that will take the next generation to a level we could only imagine."

Our legacy is our story, and it has the power to reshape our future and influence, educate and inspire others. "Embrace My Truth" is my legacy. It is a motivator and reminder of how to overcome obstacles and conquer fear and how to make a difference in this world. Decide today you are going to embrace your truth. Start by exposing your greatest fears and telling the truth. Your story is your legacy. How do you want to be remembered? It is up to you to create your narrative.

> *"Our legacy is our story, and it has the power to reshape our future and inspire others."*
> **Sasha E. Butler**

Take Action!

The Bible reassures us that embracing our truth is part of the process of overcoming our limitations:

> My grace is sufficient for you, for my power is made perfect in weakness. Therefore, I will boast all the more gladly about my weaknesses so that Christ's power may rest on me. That is why, for Christ's sake, I delight in weaknesses, in insults, in hardships, in persecutions, in difficulties. For when I am weak, then I am strong.
>
> 2 Corinthians 12:9-10, NIV

Today I encourage you to take the first steps in embracing your truth. Start writing your story, include the good and the bad things that have happened in your life. If you have already written your account, then go back and reflect on anything you have omitted. Make a list and add them to your story. **Remember, your story is your legacy! Share your story – embrace your truth!**

Reflections

1. How can I incorporate these techniques into my life, so that I can create a legacy in my family and community?

   _____

   _____

   _____

   _____

2. How will I feel if I implement these things?

   _____

   _____

   _____

   _____

3. What barriers would keep me from obtaining the thing I am working towards?

   _____

   _____

   _____

   _____

4. Who do I know that can help me to move that barrier?

_____

_____

_____

5. What do I believe about myself & is it foundationally true?

_____

_____

_____

6. Where did my beliefs come from?

_____

_____

_____

7. What would happen if I changed how or what I thought about myself?

_____

_____

_____

_____

Meet Sasha

Sasha E. Butler is a dynamic leader, international speaker, coach, minister, and master collaborator who equips leaders worldwide. She helps people reach their full potential by teaching them how to align their thinking and actions with their purpose and goals. Sasha has the unique ability to inspire people to confront and conquer their fears, identify, and deal with their character flaws, and build the confidence they need to succeed. She is in demand for her ability to help people embrace their truth and use their story as a blueprint for creating a meaningful legacy. Sasha is the CEO of the Center for Global Alliances and Leadership Expansion and a consultant at InXcellence Consulting: Training & Coaching Solutions, LLC. She is a member of the Harvard University Think Tank on Global Education and heads up an international working group with the World Council on Intercultural and Global Competence. Sasha holds a Master of Science degree in Adult Education & Human Resource Development and is currently a doctoral candidate for the degree of Doctor in Education.

Learn more about Sasha E. Butler's products and services:

Books & Blogs
www.embracemytruth.com

Speaking & Coaching
www.InxcellenceConsulting.com
sasha@InxcellenceConsulting.com

Training & Certifications
www.cgales.com | info@cgales.com

"One of the effects of fear is to disturb the senses and cause things to appear other than what they are."

Miguel de Cervantes

Inspiration From the T.O.P (Tower of Power)

Stephanie Wall

I am affectionally known as the Tower of Power by my friends and my Sorority Sisters, the Ladies of Delta Sigma Theta, Incorporated. I am confident it has everything to do with my 5'10 frame, my big personality that fills every room I enter, and my heavy sultry voice that I had to grow to love. Additionally, as I grew in confidence, my ability to be present, supporting, loving, and extremely empathic, serves to yield power.

It does not matter if you seek personal or professional development. As you seek, grow, and learn, trust the process and control what is programming your sub-conscious. Here are a few mantra's that are extremely helpful to combat the negative thoughts, energy, narratives that may be playing in your head:

- All is well, right here, right now.

- I am enough. Who I am is enough. What I do is enough, and what I have is enough.

- Don't be afraid to give up the good and go for the great

- I choose to be calm and at peace.

- I choose to love me FIRST.

- Positive energy flows to and through me.

- I create safe places, and I serve well.

- I affirm others and they affirm me.

- I gain nothing from judging others, so I choose to be non-judgmental.

- I have enough, I do enough, and I am enough.

Below are a few daily habits to form to replace those others.

- In the evening, write a list of at least 10 things, in order of importance, that must get done the next day.

- In the morning, try to complete at least 10 of things before 10 am.

- Record yourself saying your mantra aloud and listen to it throughout the day.

- Limit watching television to wind down because the subconscious mind is being programmed as you watch.

- Write a list of the 10 things that you are grateful for each morning.

- Listen to a mediation in the morning and the evening.

- Write out what your audacious goals are. I am talking about the kind of goals that you have no idea how to begin.

- Each day, right those goals out 10 times in the present tense, as if you are already doing it.

- Start operating like you already have that thing that you want.

- Take action steps towards your goal (watch the time wasters).

- Use systems to keep you organized and help you work more efficiently.

- Practice your craft.

- Get specialized training, so you will have the confidence.

- Find a group of like-minded folks in the field that you seek to grow.

- Plan to work and work the plan.

- Go where you celebrated.

- Watch those "I" and "Me" statements and instead think power, feeling and conviction. According to Les Brown, when you show up in any space, you should walk in any room looking and feeling empowered and seeking to empower others...through your conviction in an area of being exceptional.

Books to Read in Addition to This One

Overcoming the Impostor by Kris Kelso

How My Part-Time Job Saved My Life by Stephanie Wall

The New Psycho-Cybernetics by Maxwell Maltz

Any book, workshops, or training that will help you achieve your goal.

DON'T YOU QUIT

When things go wrong, as they sometimes will,
When the road you're trudging seems all uphill,
When the funds are low and the debts are high,
And you want to smile, but you have to sigh,
When care is pressing you down a bit-
Rest if you must, but don't you quit.
Life is queer with its twists and turns,
As every one of us sometimes learns,
And many a fellow turn about
When he might have won had he stuck it out.
Don't give up though the pace seems slow -
You may succeed with another blow.
Often the goal is nearer than
It seems to a faint and faltering man.
Often the struggler has given up
When he might have captured the victor's cup.
And he learned too late when the night came down,
How close he was to the golden crown.
Success is failure turned inside out -
The silver tint in the clouds of doubt,
And you never can tell how close you are,
It might be near when it seems afar.
So, stick to the fight when you are hardest hit -
It's when things seem worst that you must not quit.
AUTHOR UNKNOWN

Take Action!

Use this page to write down all the things that you are afraid of doing (example: writing a book, riding a bike, speaking in public, singing in public, etc.).

☐ _____

☐ _____

☐ _____

☐ _____

☐ _____

☐ _____

☐ _____

☐ _____

☐ _____

NOW, GO OUT AND DO EACH OF THOSE THINGS.

As you do each thing, cross it off of the list. When we do the small things that we are afraid to do, it makes it easier for us to the overcome the larger challenges that may be keeping us from our dreams.

Reflections

1. How can I incorporate these techniques into my life, so that I can create a legacy in my family and community?

_____

_____

_____

_____

2. How will I feel if I implement these things?

_____

_____

_____

_____

3. What barriers would keep me from obtaining the thing I am working towards?

_____

_____

_____

_____

4. Who do I know that can help me to move that barrier?

_____

_____

_____

5. What do I believe about myself & is it foundationally true?

_____

_____

_____

6. Where did my beliefs come from?

_____

_____

_____

7. What would happen If I changed how or what I thought about myself?

_____

_____

_____

_____

Meet Stephanie

Stephanie Wall is a passionate, Speaker, Author, and Coach who epitomizes the definition of a purpose-driven life; she is committed to advocating for women survivors of trauma. As a community change-agent who served in Law Enforcement for 20 years, with a master's degree in Business & Organizational Leadership and certifications for Transformational, Solution-based & Life Coaching. She uses empathy and an action-oriented attitude to help people combat life's challenges.

Stephanie authored "How My Part-time Job Saved My Life: A True Story of Overcoming Abuse and Claiming a Victorious Life" to demonstrate how to conquer a traumatic past. Additionally, she is the Co-Author of several of Amazon's #1 Best Sellers books. As a result of her devotion to help women, Stephanie created Speaker Stephanie LLC, a personal development brand, bridging her passion and career; from keynote speaking and hosting interactive leadership seminars, to individual and group coaching. Stephanie is a loving wife, mother, and grandmother (Gigi). She and her husband live in Maryland, USA.

You can connect with Stephanie here:
Speakerstephanie.com (website)
Speakerstephaniew (Instagram)

> *"Happiness is a by-product of helping others."*

Denny Miller

"There can be no happiness if the things we believe in are different from the things that we do."

Freya Stark

Personal Reflections

_____

_____

_____

_____

_____

_____

_____

_____

_____

_____

_____

_____

_____

_____

_____

_____

Personal Reflections

Personal Reflections

Personal Reflections

Personal Reflections

Personal Reflections

Made in the USA
Columbia, SC
29 April 2021